thankfulness

A Highly Favoured Life Devotional

Copyright © The Highly Favoured Life 2024

Published and Designed by Unmovable Publications

ALL RIGHTS RESERVED to The Highly Favoured Life and authorized writers.

No part of this book may be reproduced, transmitted, or sold in any form or by any means, electronic, or mechanical, including photocopying, recording, or by any information storage and retrieval system, without permission in writing from the publisher.

All scripture quotations are from the King James Version (KJV) of the Bible.

ISBN:
978-1-967189-14-4 (paperback)
978-1-967189-15-1 (hardback)

Table of Contents

Thank You! 7
    By Debra Birner

Thankful for His Plan 11
    By Andrea Leeder

Thankfulness Brings Peace 15
    By Rita Nichols

Thankful for His Will 19
    By Anja Meyer

Put on Your Thanksgiving Lenses! 23
    By Fabiola Haynes

Give Thanks! 27
    By Susan Hutchens

Lessons of Thankfulness from a Seed 33
    By Courtney Womack

A Spirit of Thanksgiving 37
    By Tricia Wood

Thankful for the Promises 41
    By Grace Shiflett

With Grateful Heart 45
    By Beverley Wells

Are You a Blessing to God? 51
    By Lydia Riley

The Little Things 55
    By Kay Reese

Avoid Unthankfulness 59
    By Coretta Gomes

Learning about God and Becoming Thankful . . 63
    By Emily Mariner

Praising Through Thankfulness 67
    By Lisa Petersen

Thanksliving, Not Just Thanksgiving	71
By Makayla Fehr	
Thankful... Even Through the Trials?	77
By Breanna Patton	
Thankfulness in the Life of Anna	81
By Misty Wells	
Thankfulness - A Cure for the Anxious Heart	85
By Tori Ruckman	
Being Thankful During Difficult Times	89
By Catherine Aylor	
Are You Doing A Good Job?	95
By Deborah South	
Thankful Through Trials	99
By Adaiah Byrley	
So Thankful	103
By Wanda Davidson	
Thankful for Being Left Out	107
By Kelly Byrley	
Thankful for God's Guarantees	113
By Dixie Sasser	
Thankful All the Time	117
By Julie Payne	
Effects of Thanklessness	121
By Kathy Lane	
Say, "Thank You!"	125
By Callie Payne	
Thankful for Who God Is	129
By Larissa Bell	
Giving Thanks - A Different Perspective	135
By Cherith Shiflett	
Can I Be Trusted?	139
By Victoria Kiker	

Dedication

To the ladies who have worked in ministry and served
their families faithfully, we are thankful to you
for being the Titus 2 women in our lives.
Your service to the Lord does not go unseen.

Thank You!

By Debra Birner

Every good gift and every perfect gift is from above, and cometh down from the Father of lights, with whom is no variableness, neither shadow of turning.

James 1:17

One of the things that makes me appreciate thankfulness is actually unthankfulness. There is a person to whom I used to enjoy sending gifts. I enjoyed selecting the right gifts, sending them out, and waiting to hear how much the gifts were enjoyed. Unfortunately, usually, after some time went by and I hadn't heard back, I would contact that person. I would say, "Hey did you get your gift? I sent you something." And the response would be, "Oh yeah, I got it, thanks." It was usually a nonchalant kind of thanks. It didn't seem like they were really thankful.

On the other hand, my grandson recently acquired some high-brand, expensive athletic shoes. He was very excited about these shoes, though they were secondhand. They had some red around them, and I commented to him that red shoestrings would really make them pop. He said, "Well, I don't have red shoestrings so they'll be fine like this." I ordered him some red shoe strings from Amazon. It was just a pair of shoestrings. It was not a big deal. But he was so excited and thankful. He called me, he texted me, and when he saw me, he threw his arms around me and said, "Come see my red shoestrings." It really makes me want to get him other things, because he was so thankful.

These two experiences, as I reflect upon them, help me to evaluate my own life. When someone does something small for me, I want to truly appreciate, not only the gift, but the fact that they are showing love to me through the gift or the action or the time they are investing in me. I am so very blessed that I have received small gifts and extremely generous gifts as well. God has put so many people into my life that bless me continually. And I am thankful. I'm thankful for all God does for me.

More than being thankful for the gift, I am thankful for the great Giver of all gifts. My God, my Father, my Saviour, my Friend, my Healer, my Deliverer – He is so good to me. Every good gift comes from above. The people who give me small gifts, it is a gift from above. It is my God using that person to bestow a blessing on me from God Almighty Himself. I want to always remember that every good gift is from Him.

To everyone who reads this that has ever given me a gift, I thank you. I thank you for the gift of your friendship, of your love, and of your time. And I thank God that He has put you in my life. I thank God for Himself. After all, He is the greatest gift.

thankfulness

Date:

Scripture:

I'm thankful for...

On my heart...

Thankful for His Plan

By Andrea Leeder

Enter into his gates with thanksgiving, and into his courts with praise: be thankful unto him, and bless his name.

Psalms 100:4

I'm thankful for God having better plans for us in place of the plans we have for ourselves. Sometimes, we go through life, and in our minds, we have an idea of what we think things should be like. We plan out our future thinking it should be or stay a certain way;then the Lord decides to do something different with our lives. We think our whole world has just fallen apart. When looking back, the Lord knew exactly what was best for us and knew we needed to change up some things and go a "different route" so to speak.

I'm so thankful that God's plans are not our plans. I look back at ways the Lord changed things up in my life. I can truly say I am thankful He did. I wouldn't have it any other way. He sees a bigger picture that we cannot see. It takes faith to trust that the Lord knows what He is doing.

I'm thankful that God works all things together for His good. I'm thankful that God's plans are bigger than ours. He will always carry me through, no matter what season I may be in.

Here's my challenge to you. When you're going through a time of change, try to find things you can be thankful for and enter into His gates with thanksgiving and into His courts praising Him. I have not always been thankful in the moment when going through a season of change. To be honest, it's hard to be thankful when you are hurting or discouraged, but God means it for our good. If we focus on a better ending than we had in mind, it's easier to be thankful. Thank God that He didn't let your plans be the ones that kept you from growing and reaching new heights for Him. Thank God for stretching you and getting you out of your comfort zone so you can be more useful for Him. If God is working in your life, thank Him for taking the time to mold and make you into a vessel fit for the Master's use. Be thankful for His plan over ours!

thankfulness

Date:

Scripture:

I'm thankful for...

On my heart...

Thankfulness Brings Peace

By Rita Nichols

And let the peace of God rule in your hearts, to the which also ye are called in one body: and be ye thankful.

Colossians 3:15.

I have found that when I am going through a difficult situation, I want God's peace. The peace beyond all understanding. This peace requires two major things.

First, I must accept the situation as from the hand of God; He has allowed this event to happen. It has a purpose in my life. I need to remember that the Lord loves me and is training me to be more like Him. While it is often very unpleasant to go through these times, I must be thankful that the Lord chooses to do anything in my life.

Secondly, I must trust God for the outcome. This is especially hard for me. In order to have God's peace, I must surrender to His will in this situation. I can mentally know how much God loves me, but fear and faithlessness cloud my mind, and I am consumed with anxiety. God cannot give me His peace because I have not fully trusted Him. My prayers are more like suggestions to God on how I want the situation to be rather than complete surrender to God's plan. Oh, I might tack on the phrase, "if it is your will," but I really haven't fully surrendered.

To truly have the Lord's peace, I must accept and surrender to His will. When I do this, then fear will not keep me from being thankful for how God works in my life.

I must trust God for the outcome.

thankfulness

Date:

Scripture:

I'm thankful for...

On my heart...

Thankful for His Will

By Anja Meyer

In every thing give thanks: for this is the will of God in Christ Jesus concerning you.
1 Thessalonians 5:18

It was the night before the first scan in my eighth pregnancy. Due to a previous traumatic experience, my anxiety was quickly mounting. I desperately needed the LORD's help, so my husband prayed earnestly with me that I may accept, with thankfulness, whatsoever we find on the scan in the morning.

It is wonderful when things go well; how we want it to. During these times it is easy to be thankful. We can praise God and His goodness. Others can understand how we can give glory to God. Job's question, however, is a serious one: "What? shall we receive good at the hand of God, and shall we not receive evil?" (Job 2:10b)

Sometimes we get confused, thinking that God exists for us, for our happiness, our comfort, and our prosperity. I am not trying to imply that He is not a loving Father Who wants only the best for His children, but He does explain to us in Isaiah 55:8-9, "For my thoughts are not your thoughts, neither are your ways my ways, saith the Lord. For as the heavens are higher than the earth, so are my ways higher than your ways, and my thoughts than your thoughts."

What is expected of us, is to be thankful in all things - that is the Lord's will for us. The beauty of trusting in Him, and accepting with thankfulness whatsoever He allows in our paths, is the peace, joy, and contentment that it brings. We can rest in the fact that the Lord knows what is best, that He has a plan, and a purpose for each of His children and that He promises to walk through each valley and over each mountaintop with us, step by step (Hebrews 13:5.)

By accepting each hard stretch on our paths with thankfulness, we fulfill our real purpose in this life. We exist to praise Him, to bring Him honour and glory, and to cause others to praise, honour, and glorify Him. Being thankful in the ashes, during the hardest times, is the brightest testimony to the goodness and faithfulness of the Lord (Job 1:21.)

If we struggle to find something to be thankful for in a situation, let's be thankful for the wonderful truth Paul reminded us of in Romans 8:38-39, "For I am persuaded, that neither death, nor life, nor angels, nor principalities, nor powers, nor things present, nor things to come, Nor height, nor depth, nor any other creature, shall be able to separate us from the love of God, which is in Christ Jesus our Lord."

Well, what the scan revealed to us the next morning, I never expected in my wildest dreams. The Lord had blessed us with twins! Despite so many fears and risks involved in this pregnancy, my husband and I felt overwhelming thankfulness. The Lord is always good!

thankfulness

Date:

Scripture:

I'm thankful for...

On my heart...

Put on Your Thanksgiving Lenses!

By Fabiola Haynes

Therefore will I give thanks unto thee, O LORD, among the heathen, and sing praises unto thy name.

Psalm 18:49

In this Scripture, we see the psalmist David giving thanks unto God for delivering him from his enemies, as well as from the hand of Saul. How is it that he could praise and give thanks to God while constantly being on the run and hiding in caves? Because he knew Who God was and how He was able to provide him deliverance. David could've chosen depression and simply died in a cave, but instead, he decided to look at his life through a thanksgiving lens.

It's amazing how being thankful sure changes our view of things! This is a principle that I try to keep in mind daily to help me have a better day in pleasing my Lord. When the house looks like an earthquake just took place, instead of complaining, I try to thank God I have five boys who will one day hopefully shake up a nation with the Gospel! When I feel like I should have my husband all to myself, I try to thank God that He gives him the wisdom and patience to help others have a great home and marriage like ours. When I feel like I'm overwhelmed with tasks to do, I try to thank God that He even allows me to be a part of His work! The list could go on.

Like my husband always says, "The quickest way to be miserable is to decide you're going to be." What a truth! The days I forget to put on my thanksgiving lenses are the days I look back and realize all the joy I missed with my husband, children, and walking with the Lord.

"I can complain because rose bushes have thorns or rejoice because 'thorn' bushes have roses."-Unknown

The quickest way to be miserable is to decide you're going to be.

thankfulness

Date:

Scripture:

I'm thankful for...

On my heart...

Give Thanks!

By Susan Hutchens

*O give thanks unto the LORD; call upon his name:
make known his deeds among the people.*

Psalm 105:1

God loves to hear us give thanks to Him for all He has done. We know that it's His explicit will that we give thanks to Him in all things. And in this text, we see that we should "make known his deeds among the people." We need to tell others what He has done. What has the Lord done for you? I made an acrostic of the word THANKS to tell you some of the things He's done for me.

Time - I'm thankful for time. Does that sound crazy? Benjamin Franklin said, "Time is the stuff life is made of." We aren't promised tomorrow, so we should treasure this day and show our thankfulness by using our time wisely. I'm so thankful to have time to spend with family, to serve the Lord, and to do fruitful work! My prayer is to be present and use my time purposefully.

What an amazing gift that God gives us joy and the capacity to be happy in this life!

Happiness - I thank the Lord for joy! Joy and happiness are gifts from the Lord. Ecclesiastes 2:26 tells us, "For God giveth to a man that is good in his sight wisdom, and knowledge, and joy . . . ." What an amazing gift that God gives us joy and the capacity to be happy in this life!

Access - Prayer! How wonderful that we have the privilege of going directly to our God with our problems and needs. We have the assurance that He hears us! We can come boldly to Him with our requests, and Philippians 4:6-7 tells us to pray with thanksgiving so that we might have the peace of God. I'm so thankful for direct access to my heavenly Father!

Necessities and Niceties - I'm thankful for having my needs met and also for the extras that aren't needs, but nice to have. I enjoy the deck in my backyard and drink my coffee out there after breakfast. It's not something I need, but the Lord has allowed me to have it, just for my enjoyment. I like having a cell phone. Definitely not a necessity, but so nice to have pictures of my grandchildren and good music to listen to . . . oh, and to actually call people too! We have so many things in our North American culture that we take for granted, never stopping to thank God for all the material blessings He's given us that we don't even truly need!

Kindred - I had to fit my family in there somewhere, didn't I?! I thank the Lord so much for my goodly heritage (Psalm 16:6). My parents and my husband's parents are all saved and serving the Lord faithfully. We're blessed to have our adult children serving the Lord;

what sweet fulfillment there is in seeing our children serve God! I'm so blessed to have a husband who loves me, who tenderly and faithfully cares for me. Thank God for my family!

Salvation - This greatest gift of God fills my heart as I reflect on His overwhelming love for me (Jeremiah 31:3)! I'm so thankful that over fifty years ago, God saved my dad and changed our family's direction. I was saved many years later, but I'm thankful for that beginning and my childhood years spent in a godly home. I'm thankful that God never let me rest until I made my salvation sure. I love that sweet assurance in my soul that I am a child of God!

These are just a few of the things I'm thankful for, but I wanted to make some of God's glorious deeds known among the people today! What are you thankful for today? How can you make it known among the people?

thankfulness

Date:

Scripture:

I'm thankful for...

On my heart...

Lessons of Thankfulness from a Seed

By Courtney Womack

And he said unto me, My grace is sufficient for thee: for my strength is made perfect in weakness. Most gladly therefore will I rather glory in my infirmities, that the power of Christ may rest upon me.

II Corinthians 12:9

Have you ever nurtured a garden or watched flowers bloom from seeds? It's a process of patience and care, from preparing the soil to pulling weeds and tending the plants. However, there is something we can't shield our plants from – the struggle of growth. A few months back, my daughter excitedly planted some sunflower seeds. As they began to sprout, she noticed some struggling to shed their seed casings. She worried they might wither or remain stunted, unable to break free from their old shells. Because of my love and time spent gardening, I cautioned her not to interfere. I explained that, despite our instincts to ease their struggle, it's crucial for seedlings to overcome challenges independently - just as it is for us. Life often presents us with hardships and trials. We may feel burdened, wondering why we must endure such challenges.

It's in these moments that we must pause and be thankful for the process. Like those sunflowers, our struggles serve to strengthen and fortify us, shaping us into resilient servants of God, capable of weathering life's storms.

As a gardener, I've come to be thankful for the resilience gained from overcoming obstacles.

As a follower of Christ, I've learned to embrace trials as opportunities for spiritual growth. It's not about denying the difficulty or even loving it. (Because, let's be honest, trials are not fun!) But acknowledging that every experience, whether pleasant or painful, contributes to our journey of faith (I Corinthians 15:57-58; II Corinthians 12:9-10).

In the words of Andrew Murray, "I am here by God's appointments, in His timing, under His training, for His time." Each trial, each adversity, has a purpose – whether to strengthen our faith or to reveal God's glory to the world. In I Thessalonians 5:18, we are reminded "in every thing give thanks." Even in the midst of adversity, like Jonah in the belly of the fish, we can offer a voice of thanksgiving for our situation of struggle, pain, or trial. Though our situation may seem dire, we should trust in God's sovereignty and plan, knowing that He will work all things for His good. So, as you navigate life's challenges, remember to cultivate a spirit of gratitude. Whether you find yourself in the depths of a valley or on the mountaintop, cherish the growth process. For it's through adversity that we truly learn to appreciate life's blessings and to be thankful.

thankfulness

Date:

Scripture:

I'm thankful for...

On my heart...

A Spirit of Thanksgiving

By Tricia Wood

*Giving thanks always for all things unto God
and the father in the name of our Lord Jesus Christ;*

Ephesians 5:20

What if you woke up tomorrow morning with only the things you thanked God for today?

I am so glad that we as Americans have a national holiday set aside for the giving of thanks. Even still, I wonder how many people truly make time during that special holiday to express their gratitude. We are losing our spirit of Thanksgiving as we are surrounded by a society that is selfish and entitled. One who expects special treatment does not appreciate the time, effort, or money it took to give them that special treatment. I'm sure we all know someone who tends to be that way. It is not a pleasure to do anything for them. We all want to feel appreciated. We also want gratitude expressed to us.

I wonder if this is how God feels toward us. How often do I just expect Him to do things for me without any appreciation or gratitude coming from my heart or mouth? Do I spend as much time thanking Him for what He's already done as I do pouring out my prayer request? As our verse says, "Giving thanks always for all things unto God." Lord, help me not to be selfish, entitled, and ungrateful. Help me to express my gratitude to others and to you. My prayer is to continually have a spirit of thanksgiving all year through.

Lord, help me to express my gratitude to you.

thankfulness

Date:

Scripture:

I'm thankful for...

On my heart...

Thankful for the Promises

By Grace Shiflett

For all the promises of God in him are yea, and in him Amen, unto the glory of God by us.

II Corinthians 1:20

I am so thankful for the Word of God. I am privileged, as are many of you, to own several copies of the Bible. The guide to all we will face in this life. The older I get, the more I realize how much I have learned to examine and depend on the many promises found in God's Word! The more you rely on them and run to His Word to find them, the more it will become second nature to hold fast to them. I'm thankful that His promises are tried and true. No matter what we are facing, we can rest and rejoice in the sure promises. I am thankful for the Scripture we have been given to sustain us in this life. Here are a few taken from the same book in the Bible.

"...With men this is impossible; but with God all things are possible."
- Matthew 19:26b

"Ask, and it shall be given you; seek, and ye shall find; knock, and it shall be opened unto you."
- Matthew 7:7

"Heaven and earth shall pass away, but my words shall not pass away."
- Matthew 24;35

The list of God's promises could go on and on. Go read them, embrace them, walk in them, and mostly thank God for them. So many wonderful promises are given to us through His Word. As we get close to the Lord's return, let's fill our hearts and minds with His promises. They will be our lifeline as we navigate through all the ups and downs of life. Stand on His promises. Remind yourself often of these promises.

I'm thankful that His promises are tried and true.

thankfulness

Date:

Scripture:

I'm thankful for...

On my heart...

With Grateful Heart

By Beverley Wells

In every thing give thanks: for this is the will of God in Christ Jesus concerning you.
I Thessalonians 5:18

Have you ever found yourself in such a state of thankfulness that it truly becomes overwhelming? So much to the point that you don't have the words to explain yourself? You are swept away with such humbleness, gratitude, and elation that you wish time would stand still. I desire that each of you would experience gratitude to that degree.

I'm guessing that depends upon time and age. When one is younger, somehow life seems to just pass you by because you are filled with energy and youth. As you mature in age and wisdom, you tend to appreciate things in a new light and the reality of life's blessings. I'm not speaking as "one who has arrived." I too, stand in need of a more grateful and thankful heart. I find the answer to a grateful heart comes when we apply the Word in our life. I Thessalonians 5:18 says, "In every thing give thanks: for this is the will of God in Christ Jesus concerning you." Being thankful may not change the situation, but it sure changes how you react and respond to what life brings your way.

I find the answer to a grateful heart comes when we apply the Word in our life.

Being thankful can be one of the hardest things to learn. We are such a blessed nation and group of people that we often think we stand in need of nothing. This attitude has sadly developed an unthankful spirit in the best of us. An unthankful nation will be a forsaken nation. We must consciously make a point to be thankful. May we learn to be thankful before what we take for granted is removed from our lives.

Even when we find ourselves in the deepest of valleys, we can find something to be thankful for:

The very breath that we breathe is not ours. It is given to us and we give it no thought. For this, I am thankful.

The sun sets and rises bringing in a new day. I am thankful!

I have eyes that can see, feet that can walk, a voice to talk. I am thankful!

I have food on my table and shoes on my feet. I am thankful!

I have a roof over my head. I am thankful!

I have a husband and family that I love and they love me. I am thankful!

I have a church and place where I can serve the Lord. I am thankful!

This list could no doubt go on and on. Start a list of things that you are thankful for and make the declaration that you are thankful. Then, you will quickly begin to experience a heart of overwhelming gratitude that brings you into a deeper relationship with the Lord unlike any other. This is an emotional and spiritual place to be: a place of solitude, peace, and calm; a place of rest and restoration; a place of healing and help.

When you experience this place, it seems as if time stands still and you would love to stay there just a while longer. Oftentimes, I feel as if I am that half-breed baby in Ezekiel 16, who was left to die in her own blood, but then Jesus passed by my way, took me in His arms, and said, "Live!" For this, I am most thankful!

If you have never found this place and it sounds inviting, realize that it must be entered into by a heart of gratitude and thankfulness. With pen in hand, begin your list of the things that you have and know in your life. State it, then write, "I am thankful!" Begin with a goal to write 10 things and speak it, I am thankful! Quote I Thessalonians 5:18.

I simply cannot describe the relationship that you will find in the Lord when you submit to His will and His working in and through you. It is beyond words. It's like trying to describe the birth of a child to someone who has never had the privilege. You have to experience it yourself. I promise you it's worth it. It surpasses any love that you could ever have in this life, even that of loving your husband and your children. For me, I can't imagine loving anyone more than my husband or my children. I have told them they are the reason I live, yet the Lord is the breath that I breathe. May I keep my relationship right with Him by having a Spirit-controlled life and a never-dying heart of gratitude. For Thee, my Lord, I am thankful!

Other reading:
Psalm 136:1, I Chronicles 16:34, Psalm 9:1-2,
Psalm 86:12, Psalm 28:7, I Samuel 12:24

thankfulness

Date:

Scripture:

I'm thankful for...

On my heart...

Are You a Blessing to God?

By Lydia Riley

Bless the Lord, O my soul, and forget not all his benefits:

Psalm 103:2

This verse is often used on church bulletins and banners for the Thanksgiving season, but in reality, an attitude of thankfulness should permeate our hearts and our homes every day of the year. We know that the Lord blesses our lives in so many ways – and loads us with His benefits. Just as a job may offer great benefits to entice their employees, our God offers unbelievable benefits in the Christian life – He forgives! He redeems! He satisfies! He is merciful and gracious! He knows us! He remembers us! These are some of the benefits the Psalmist rejoices in throughout the rest of this chapter as he reflects on the many benefits of our Saviour.

But let's look at the first part of the verse about blessing the Lord. This is a direct command from the Psalmist to his own soul, the very core of who he is, to "bless" the Lord. This amazes me that we could actually be a blessing to the God of Heaven, the Creator of the Universe, the One who knows all, sees all, and has all. When sharing how the Lord has blessed us, we often speak of the beauty, happiness, contentment, and pleasure that He pours into our lives. Does the Lord look upon my life and my soul, the core of all I really am, as bringing Himself beauty, happiness, contentment, and pleasure?

We are blessed to be a blessing! Let's return the love and favor He has given us in ceaseless worship and praise, and live our lives where He can look upon us and say, "My child, you are a blessing to me!"

Bless the Lord, O my soul!

> An attitude of thankfulness should permeate our hearts and our homes every day of the year.

thankfulness

Date:

Scripture:

I'm thankful for...

On my heart...

The Little Things

By Kay Reese

Giving thanks always for all things....

Ephesians 5:20

Someone once said that all the little things make up the big. In the beginning of a poem I recently read, it humbly asks, "Dear God, please give to me a thankful heart for the little things." As Christians, it is a natural attribute to be grateful for all the Lord has done and is doing in our lives. Unfortunately, there are times we overlook the little things. I know I do more than I care to say.

Don't get me wrong, each day I am overjoyed that God allowed me to be born in a land where I am free. He let me hear the gospel and be saved by His grace. He not only wants me to appreciate the greater but the smaller things also, no matter how insignificant they seem to be. The poem mentioned things like the joy of family celebrations, the little mundane jobs we do each day, and creation's changing of the seasons.

Then I began to think of other things, like all the little ones He has brought my way. My own children, my grandchildren, the kids in my church, or the youth in my community. Each one is precious to Jesus and I am to appreciate them and be an example of His love.

Also, I thought of how God takes notice of all things. He cares when a little sparrow falls (Matthew 10:29.) I am to show my gratefulness for His caring for every little detail of my life. He is concerned about whatever touches me! He wants me to be excited each time I gather together with others in His name, even if it's only a few, He is in the midst of us (Matthew 18:20.) I am to acknowledge my thankfulness when He may take a simple song's words and bring healing to my hurting heart. Someone may utter a little prayer and the words of it miraculously bring faith to me in a difficult time. God will use His servant to deliver a message from His Word that will project a small light to make my pathway clear. Yes, these are little things to appreciate! The end of the poem mentioned before says, "Let me love the little things I find along the way."

thankfulness

Date:

Scripture:

I'm thankful for...

On my heart...

Avoid Unthankfulness

By Coretta Gomes

Yea, they turned back and tempted God, and limited the Holy One of Israel. They remembered not his hand, nor the day when he delivered them from the enemy.

Psalm 78:41-42

What an unthankful generation we live in. Our nation is full of people who have no idea what our forefathers went through for us to enjoy the freedoms we have. Grumbling and outrage about one's rights results in a country full of rioting, selfishness, sinful living, and crime. How did we get here so fast? One of the reasons is an unthankful generation. How can we avoid unthankfulness? In God's Word, through the nation of Israel, we can observe a few ways to avoid unthankfulness.

The Israelites ceased to obey God's command to tell their children and children's children of God's salvation. He brought them out of Egypt and saved them from a life of slavery. Just like God saved the Israelites, He saved us from sin and a life of slavery to sin. We are gloriously saved and on our way to heaven. What a wonderful freedom we have in Christ! How often do we remind our children of the salvation we have in Christ and thank the Lord for dying on the cross for our sin? The Israelites ceased to remind their children and those around them of God's salvation. Do not forget where God brought you from. Don't be unthankful for His salvation.

The Israelites ceased to tell their children and children's children about the protection God had given them. He protected them countless times in the wilderness: parted the Red Sea allowing them to go over on dry land, caused the Egyptian army to perish in that same sea the moment the Israelites had all crossed over, and gave them victory battle after battle. How often do we remind our children or others of the times the Lord protected us from an accident or even when in an accident? I can recall many times God protected me as a child and throughout my adult life from or in an accident. Do we share these times of God's protection with our children and others? What about your personal victories? Personally, I could fill page after page of victories God allowed me to have, and am sure you could as well. Share your victories!

The Israelites ceased to share with their children and children's children the many blessings of God. He shielded them with a cloud from the hot, wilderness days, provided a warm fire by night, clothes and shoes never wore out and grew with them (amazing!), gave them manna from above, and provided water (never hungering or thirsting). What a miracle! Yet the Israelites forgot all these wonderful blessings. Do not forget to contemplate and share with others the blessings the Lord has done for you, however small they may be. Be thankful for God's blessings in your life.

Unthankfulness comes when we forget and do not share God's salvation, protection, and blessings in our lives. We have much to be thankful for! Be a woman of thankfulness. Share with your children and others the salvation, protection, and blessings of the Lord which will result in a thankful heart! "That the generation to come might know them, even the children which should be born; who should arise and declare them to their children. That they might set their hope in God, and not forget the works of God, but keep his commandments" Psalm 78:6-7.

thankfulness

Date:

Scripture:

I'm thankful for...

On my heart...

Learning about God and Becoming Thankful

By Emily Mariner

I will love thee, O LORD, my strength. The LORD is my rock, and my fortress, and my deliverer; my God, my strength, in whom I will trust; my buckler, and the horn of my salvation, and my high tower. I will call upon the LORD, who is worthy to be praised....

Psalm 18:1-3

My family moved to our mission field with very little other than the essentials. The rest of our belongings were in boxes that would take a couple of months to ship to us. Soon after we moved, I began to be discontent. I started to meditate on Matthew 6, but it was hard and that didn't seem to help. I knew God had supplied everything, and I was writing lists and praying for the things that God had done. But it still wasn't renewing my mind. In November, I wanted my Thanksgiving décor, but worked on being thankful for the things I had. But then Christmas came, starting the whole process over.

During this time, I was reading through the Psalms, and I kept seeing a continuous theme throughout them. Especially in the Psalms by David, it would often begin with a struggle or problem and then end with praising God. But it wasn't praising God because He fixed the problem. It was praising God for Who He is. Psalm 18 was written after David was delivered from Saul. David starts the chapter by describing the character of God. Read Psalm 18:1-2. God had saved David, but David didn't start there. He started by recognizing Who God is. He is my strength. He is my rock. God was able to deliver David because He is able. God is able because He is the all-powerful Creator God. Of course, the God who created everything could save a man who was being hunted by an army.

As I meditated on this thought, I went to Philippians 4. Paul states that he learned how to be content in whatever state he was in. It is evident that he truly did, as we can see in Acts 16. In Acts 16, Paul was in prison, praying, and singing praises to God. In prison. How could he do this? How did he learn to praise in such circumstances? Unfortunately, Paul doesn't give an exact formula or step-by-step plan. Instead, he says simply, "I can do all things through Christ which strengtheneth me" (Philippians 4:13.)

This verse suddenly clicked in my head. The only way I can do anything is by God enabling me. The only way I can truly be thankful is to realize I can't on my own, but I can by realizing this ability comes from my God. I'm not perfect, nor will I ever be. This will be a lifelong pursuit. My circumstances will change. My attitude will change. God never changes. When I shift my focus off of my circumstances and onto my own attitude of God and Who He is, then I can become truly thankful.

thankfulness

Date:

Scripture:

I'm thankful for...

On my heart...

Praising Through Thankfulness

By Lisa Petersen

Enter into his gates with thanksgiving, and into his courts with praise: be thankful unto him, and bless his name.

Psalm 100:4

Many of us have heard this verse for our whole life and probably have it memorized. But do we do it every day? He is worthy! Thankfulness is a state of mind. We can be thankful for different things at different times, but being in a state of thankfulness should always be in our heart and mind. It tells us that our heart is right with the Lord, and we are looking to Him for our help, not looking at our circumstances. The Lord always wants us to be full of thankfulness. Does that mean even going through trials? Yes, it does. It is tough, but that is what God wants. He wants us to praise Him, even when our heart is hurting.

There are so many ways to thank and praise God. All we have to do is go to the Psalms to see how David praised Him, even going through the most stressful of times. God wants us to praise and thank Him in all seasons of our life. What are some things we can always be in a state of thankfulness about?

1. God will always take care of His own. It might not be how you think it should be done, but He will take care of you.
2. God answers prayers.
3. God gives us daily provisions.
4. God gives us friends and family.
5. God keeps His promises. Whatever He says, He does.
6. God is always working. Even in difficult times, God is at work. We tend to think He isn't when we can't see anything happening.
7. God has prevailed and is prevailing over every enemy.
8. God is faithful.
9. God is righteous.
10. God is merciful.
11. God is longsuffering.
12. God is trustworthy.
13. God sent Jesus to die for our sins to give us eternal life.

And the list could go on . . .

I looked up the word "thankfulness" in the Bible to see how many times it was there and how it was used. It is used only one time and that is in Acts 24:3. We see there that Tertullus, who is Paul's enemy, is seeking to lift up Felix against Paul, so he praises and thanks Felix for the work that he has done for their nation. Now, if an unsaved man can praise and be full of thankfulness for a wicked ruler, how much more should we as Christians praise and be full of thankfulness for what God has done and is doing in our lives? There is a saying that I have heard many times and it is: "There is always something to be thankful for." So let's be in a state of thankfulness always and prove to people how great our God is.

thankfulness

Date:

Scripture:

I'm thankful for...

On my heart...

Thanksliving, Not Just Thanksgiving

By Makayla Fehr

As ye have therefore received Christ Jesus the Lord, so walk ye in him: rooted and built up in him, and stablished in the faith, as ye have been taught, abounding therein with thanksgiving.

Colossians 2:6-7

So many times we are not as thankful as we should be for the little things in life. We notice when big things happen, and those things mean so much to us. But what about things in life that are "small"? What about the fact that we have running water, electricity, and AC? I should be especially grateful since I live in Texas! Growing up on the mission field, I thought many things were just normal and a part of life, like running out of water mid-shower, the water being cold or having to go to the market to get our vegetables. The list could go on. Now that I am married and living in the States, I'm like, "Wow! As Americans, we are so spoiled!" I mean, let's talk about curbside pickup for groceries. You just drive up and pop your trunk. They already did the shopping for you and even loaded it

If you're truly thankful for someone, make sure to show it to them.

up in your car. The shower water is always the perfect temperature you want. You drive up and pick up any kind of food you want! Over the last few years, it's just made me realize that I'm for sure not as thankful as I should be for what the Lord has given me!

Say It

This is super simple, but let's make sure every single day we thank the Lord for His goodness to us and everything He has given us – from waking up in a king-size bed, to the warm shower, to walking up to a refrigerator full of food, etc.... I also think about the authority that God has placed over our lives for a reason. When was the last time we took a moment to tell them thank you for serving God, being a godly example, and following the Lord's leading in their lives? Take the time today to tell someone you love and respect how thankful you are for them.

Show It

There are many ways we can show how thankful we are to others. You don't always have to buy something. A simple "thank you" note or even text would mean a lot to someone you care about. For me, now that I am a mom, it makes my day when my little two-year-old thanks me for the food and gives me a big hug. Wow! Look how something so simple can go so far. If you're truly thankful for someone, make sure to show it to them. We can show how thankful we are to the Lord by serving Him, following His commandments and telling others about Him and how He died to save us.

Sincerity

It is so easy to casually say, "Oh yeah, thanks." When was the last time you said "thank you" and meant it with your whole heart? We can go through the motions of saying thank you because it was the way our mama raised us. But we need to be sincere when we say it. Do you actually mean it when you tell your spouse thank you for waking up at 5 a.m. every morning to work 40 hours a week providing for your family, the sacrifices he makes so your family is taken care of? Or when you're walking out of classes for the day, it's a casual habit to say thank you to the teacher, but she took time out of her day to study, prepare, and come to teach a whole bunch of teenagers who weren't in the least bit interested in what she had to say. Mean it when you say it!

We should be known as thankful people all the time everywhere, no matter the circumstance, whether good or bad. There is always something we can be thankful for. My challenge to you is not to just be thankful sometimes, but to live your life sincerely saying and showing thankfulness for everything.

thankfulness

Date:

Scripture:

I'm thankful for...

On my heart...

Thankful...
Even Through the Trials?

By Breanna Patton

In every thing give thanks: for this is the will of God in Christ Jesus concerning you.

I Thessalonians 5:18

That I may publish with the voice of thanksgiving, and tell of all thy wondrous works.

Psalm 26:7

Does it ever feel like you are hit with trial after trial? Like you are getting beat by wave after wave and you can't come up for air? It's often during these trials in our lives that the Lord grows us and shows His strength through us. How can we stay thankful during these trying times in our lives?

1. It's not an option. You mean I have to be thankful through these trials and storms of life? Yes! I Thessalonians 5:18 says, "In every thing give thanks; for this is the will of God in Christ Jesus concerning you." We are commanded to give thanks in everything, not just in "some" things or when things are going our way. Every trial and storm in life

has a purpose in making us more like Christ. So, let's be thankful in all things.

2. Recognize He can be glorified through our hard times. Psalm 26:7 says, "That I may publish with the voice of thanksgiving, and tell of all thy wondrous works." Wow! This verse tells us that we may (or get to) publish all the things that He does for us. We get to be a great testimony to the world around us by looking at our seemingly never-ending trials as a way to praise and worship our Creator.

3. Give Him praise when something goes wrong. You have a flat tire? Thank Him, as He may have just saved you from getting into a car accident. Have a sickness or an illness that seems like it will never go away? Thank Him for His strength to help you recover or get through it. You have a toddler throwing a tantrum in the middle of the grocery store? Thank Him for that precious little one that He has given you to raise, even though your patience may be running thin and you're weary.

My husband just recently totaled his "new to him" pickup truck that we had just paid off. An elderly lady had run a red light and pulled in front of him. He had no way of stopping as he was also pulling our church's tractor on a trailer. My first response was, "God, why did you allow this to happen?" But then I couldn't help but be thankful that no one was hurt. Yes, we went from a paid-off vehicle that we had only had for 9 months to no vehicle at all, but my husband and the elderly lady were both unharmed. We can look at every circumstance in life and complain about the problem, or we can choose thankfulness at how good God is to us even through the trials of life. You can choose thankfulness today!

thankfulness

Date:

Scripture:

I'm thankful for...

On my heart...

Thankfulness in the Life of Anna

By Misty Wells

And she coming in that instant gave thanks likewise unto the Lord, and spake of him to all them that looked for redemption in Jerusalem.

Luke 2:38

The adoration of Anna in the Bible is a beautiful picture of true thankfulness. Joseph and Mary have brought Jesus to the temple to fulfill the custom of the law, and there, Simeon awaits. He has been led there by the Spirit of God. It was confirmed to him that he should not see death until he has seen the Lord's Christ. Not only does he see Jesus, but he has the great privilege of holding Him in his arms. Simeon begins to exalt the Lord. He acknowledges who He is, and what He will do. He calls Him a light to lighten the Gentiles, and the glory of the people of Israel.

Then comes sweet Anna. She is a widow who has been serving night and day in the temple since the death of her husband. The Bible says of Anna in Luke 2:38, "And she coming in that instant gave thanks likewise unto the Lord, and spake of him to all them that looked for redemption in Jerusalem." The word "thanks" in this verse is derived from the Greek word "anthomologeomai," which means to "acknowledge fully, to celebrate fully in praise with thanksgiving." To "acknowledge" means "to accept or admit the existence or truth of." Another definition is "to recognize the fact or importance or quality of." Anna is giving thanks by recognizing who the Lord is and what He will do. She is acknowledging the fact that He is the Saviour of their people. She doesn't stop there. The Bible says that she speaks of Him to all those who were looking for redemption in Jerusalem. This acknowledgment and recognition is shared with those around her.

In looking at the expression of thanks in the life of Anna, we should be encouraged to fully acknowledge the giver and the gift. We should recognize who they are and what they have done. This type of gratitude affects more than them. It allows the receiver to be aware of the depths one has gone through to give. We should consider the sacrifice and effort put forth, and we should share it with others.

Have you openly acknowledged the givers in your life? Do you recognize the sacrifices and labor put forth on your behalf? Most importantly, do you realize what our Lord has done for you? Have you acknowledged the greatest Giver and gift of all? There are many around us looking for redemption. In our gratitude, we must tell them about Jesus. Let us learn from Anna and truly give thanks.

thankfulness

Date:

Scripture:

I'm thankful for...

On my heart...

Thankfulness - A Cure for the Anxious Heart

By Tori Ruckman

Be careful for nothing; but in everything by prayer and supplication with thanksgiving let your requests be made known unto God. And the God of peace, which passeth all understanding, shall keep your hearts and minds through Christ Jesus.

Philippians 4:6-7

The word careful simply means "anxious." In the day in which we live, many people have anxiety in some form or another. Let me start by saying – even real Christians have real anxiety. Being saved, truly trying to live for the Lord, and even enjoying our Christian service does not make us immune to the daily "cares" we experience. Yet, in these verses, we find a powerful weapon! As Christians, we do not have to give in to a life filled with anxiety.

As verse 6 continues, we see that the key to being "careful for nothing" is prayer and supplication;simply taking the things we are anxious about to the Lord andmaking them known unto Him. Aren't you glad we can take everything to Him, no matter how big or small?

However, it does not end with just praying about our problems. We are told to do this "with thanksgiving." How many times do we bring our worries to the Lord in prayer because we know it is the right thing to do, then get up and find ourselves right back in the same place of carefulness?

The key to gaining victory and experiencing the promise of peace "that passes all understanding" in verse 7 is not only to bring these anxieties to God but to do so with thankfulness. Why? Because being thankful amid anxiety places the focus back on God and off of our problems. It is hard to be full of care when you remember all God has done for you and Who He is!

Peace and security come when we take our worries and cares to Him with a heart of gratitude. You may be faced with a battle of anxiety like you have never faced before. The enemy loves an anxious Christian. He can use our anxiety to steer our thought life (and eventually our actions) away from the Truth. Yet, as much as the world, the flesh, and the devil love an anxious Christian, they hate even more a prayerful and thankful one. Sisters, we have every reason to choose the victory Christ has provided for us. After all, we have already won the war!

So why not try it? Have you taken your cares to Him today? Still feel the anxiety gripping your heart? Maybe try again using your weapon of thankfulness! No matter what we face He has been so good to us! In the "everythings" of life, we can give thanks (I Thessalonians 5:18.)

thankfulness

Date:

Scripture:

I'm thankful for...

On my heart...

Being Thankful During Difficult Times

By Catherine Aylor

In everything give thanks: for this is the will of God in Christ Jesus concerning you.
1 Thessalonians 5:18

When we think about being thankful, we often think about the season of Thanksgiving. This is when many people think about spending time with family and friends, having good food, helping others who are less fortunate, and many other scenarios. What about being thankful during or even being thankful for difficult times? That is not always easy to do. It may sometimes be easy for others to say when it is not their difficulty, but how do we handle difficult times with a thankful spirit?

Look at the word everything in our verse above. I have always been told or have heard, "The perfect place to be is in the center of His will." So, if the center of His will is the perfect place to be, and we are supposed to be giving thanks for everything; it must be possible to make it through the difficult times while still being thankful.

If you want to know how to be thankful in difficult times — use thankfulness like faith.

Recently we have experienced death of a great magnitude. My husband lost his oldest brother in April of 2023, and it was unexpected. We were just starting to get back to some kind of normality because it was up to us to handle since he wasn't married and didn't have any children to do so. We had a planned mission trip with our church to the Navajo Nation in August of that same year. We were so excited as we had never been on a mission trip. The trip arrived and my husband, son, and I were among almost 60 who would attend this trip. We flew in and then drove quite a distance to get to where we would be staying. It had been a very long day and trip, not to mention I had lost my computer along the way. That morning when I woke, I received a devastating message that my other brother-in-law, only one year older than my husband, was found deceased in his home. I could continue the story, but to say the least, it was difficult. We had a decision to make; to go home or stay. We decided to decide on the service that evening. God's prudence to do so was the best decision. We heard two amazing messages that solidified our stay.

This ability to do so increased our faith as well as others who were watching how we were going to handle our "...in everything give thanks..."

We were thankful God gave us the funds to be able to go. We were thankful God allowed us the opportunity to do it as a family. We were thankful other believers so many miles from home along with our church family rallied around my husband in support and prayer. We were thankful we got to walk the streets and help reach people who were hurt by drugs, alcohol, and other things that had once controlled my brother-in-law's life in years past who had just passed away. We were thankful this happened after our arrival because had it happened before we wouldn't have gone on the mission trip. We were thankful for the man whom my husband got to lead to the Lord on the last day on the last street we knocked on before heading back home. We were thankful when we arrived and had to go to my brother-in-law's home. He had his Bible, a tract, and a daily devotional book opened on the day he passed away.

If you want to know how to be thankful in difficult times—use thankfulness like faith. Each measure of faith you are given increases the next measure of faith needed for the harder things in the future. "In everything give thanks" starts with the small things, and you can remember those things to help you be thankful in the difficult "times" because with God everything is "multiplied"!

thankfulness

Date:

Scripture:

I'm thankful for...

On my heart...

Are You Doing A Good Job?

By Deborah South

And he appointed certain of the Levites to minister before the ark of the Lord, and to record, and to thank and praise the Lord God of Israel:

I Chronicles 16:4

In recent months, I have heard several sermons about our talents, gifts, and service that we should have and use for the Lord. Most of the time, we think of these as preaching, teaching, singing, playing instruments, etc. People are often confused about what their talent or talents could be.

These messages were on my mind when I began studying about thankfulness and thanksgiving. Several verses caught my attention. In I Chronicles 16, King David has just brought the ark of God to the city of Jerusalem and to the house of God. There is much excitement and gladness in this event. In verse 4, David appointed certain people " . . . to thank and praise the Lord . . . ." Wow, what a job to be given at the house of God! They were to be thankful. That was their appointed job.

If you study a bit further, you will see in II Chronicles 31:2, that King Hezekiah also appointed people " . . . to give thanks, and to praise in the gates . . . ." Look a bit more and you will find in Nehemiah 12:8, " . . . Moreover the Levites: . . . which was over the thanksgiving . . . ." Nehemiah 12:31, " . . . and appointed two great companies of them that gave thanks . . . ." Nehemiah 12:40, " . . . So stood the two companies of them that gave thanks in the house of God . . . ." In all of these verses, we see people who had a great and noble job for the Lord. They were to give thanks to God. They were appointed to give thanks. I am amazed when I think that King David, King Hezekiah, and Nehemiah looked around to find those people who they knew would take this job of thanking God seriously.

When we start truly thanking God, several things happen as seen in I Chronicles 16.
1. We make known the deeds of God, v. 8
2. We rejoice in the greatness of God, v. 9-10
3. We seek Him, v. 11
4. We remember His works of old, v. 12
5. We remember His works in the present, v. 17-23
6. We testify of Him, v. 24-32
7. We look forward to the future and His coming, v. 33

It seems that the more you thank God for, the more you find to be thankful for; it just expands! Are you doing a good job?

thankfulness

Date:

Scripture:

I'm thankful for...

On my heart...

Thankful Through Trials

By Adaiah Byrley

...the LORD gave, and the LORD hath taken away; blessed be the name of the LORD.

Job 1:21b

Have you ever had that kind of Sunday morning when nothing seems to be going right? First, you oversleep, then you burn your fingers making breakfast. You go try to ease the pain with cold water and aloe, just to come back to a burnt pan of food. Your mind is at ease when you realize you have just enough time to make a cup of coffee . . . just to spill it all over your new white dress as soon as you pull into the church parking lot! Your eyes start to tear up as you say, "Could my day get any worse?"

I know these illustrations may be a little silly, but think about the "trial" that you are facing right now in your life. Have you felt like God would never answer your prayers and take away the pain you're going through? Or have you thought, this trial will never end, I have nothing to be thankful for? That is exactly what the devil wants. The devil is very good at making us feel like everything is against us when we face a small "trial" in our lives. Any time I start to have a pity party and believe the devil's lies, God will bring back to my remembrance the story of Job.

Job was a very wealthy man. He had a wife, seven sons, three daughters, seven thousand sheep, three thousand camels, five hundred yoke of oxen, and five hundred she asses. The Bible says he was the greatest of all the men in the East. He was perfect and upright, he feared God and eschewed evil. The Lord blessed Job and put a hedge of protection around all that he had. The devil did not like this; he wanted to see Job sin. So, God allowed the devil to take away all that he had, but Job did not curse God. Instead, Job had so much integrity, that even when he lost everything he had, he still said, " . . . the LORD gave, and the LORD hath taken away; blessed be the name of the LORD" (Job 1:21.)

How amazing would it be if we could have the same testimony as Job had. There may come a day when we lose everything and everyone we love, but here is something you can be thankful if you have trusted Christ as your Saviour, you can never lose your salvation. So, let's stop being bitter about the trials we face (big or small) and thank God for His wonderful gift of salvation.

thankfulness

Date:

Scripture:

I'm thankful for...

On my heart...

So Thankful

By Wanda Davidson

Only fear the Lord, and serve Him in truth with all your heart: for consider how great things he hath done for you.

I Samuel 12:24

The prophet Samuel commands us to consider, ponder, and meditate on the great things that God has done for us. For those of us who are Americans, we have been blessed by God to be born in the greatest nation on earth. Even with her many faults, we have been so blessed! She was founded by men who had a vision of a country where men could worship God freely, provide for their families, and enjoy the beauty and bountifulness provided by our Heavenly Father. I Samuel 2:30 says, " . . . Them that honour me I will honour . . . ." How blessed I am to have lived my life in the "reaping days" of those godly seeds sown by our forefathers!

Considering further, not only was I born in America, but I was born into a Christian family. My parents set the standards for life. Sunday was the Lord's day! Settled! Work was a privilege, and God always provided enough. Morals, kindness to others, contentment, and trusting God were mainly taught by example. Oh, what peace and security I have enjoyed because of my parents' godly example!

Considering again, as a six-year old little girl, I was born into the family of God. Oh happy day when God took all my sins away! Words are not adequate to describe the difference that God has made in my life. How can I not be thankful when I consider all of the heartache that He has kept me from and all of the blessings that He has brought into my life as a child of God? Rich beyond measure both in this life and in eternity!

Samuel began the verse with the command to fear God and serve Him. I have heard it said that to serve the President of the United States would be an honor, but we act as if serving Christ is a sacrifice. No! The greatest honor ever given was the privilege of serving God. Being born again keeps you out of hell, but it also puts a divine calling upon your life. I am amazed that God would use sinners saved by His grace to accomplish His will on earth. God allows us to be a part of the great work that He wants to do in every heart. An encouraging word may keep someone from quitting, a tract may bring someone to the saving knowledge of Christ, and a godly example may influence another generation to live for Christ. When we consider the great things He has done for us, we cannot help but be thankful for His blessings and excited to bring others to Him.

thankfulness

Date:

Scripture:

I'm thankful for...

On my heart...

Thankful for Being Left Out

By Kelly Byrley

But the Lord is faithful, who shall stablish you, and keep you from evil.

2 Thessalonians 3:3

Have you ever been in a situation where you felt left out? I am confident that your answer was yes. How do I know this? Because we have all felt the sting of being left out by family, friends, co-workers, or even church members. This doesn't just happen to children and teenagers, it happens to adults, too. That pain is raw, and it's real. If we're not careful, it can cause some serious self-esteem and bitterness issues. The good news is that no matter if you're an adult or a teenager, the same thought can help soothe that sting and heal those wounds.

Did you know that sometimes being left out could actually be the Lord's protection? I can remember a time years ago when my husband and I felt left out of a group of couples at our church. We were around the same age, had many things in common, and had children around the same ages. We served in the same ministries. We got along well with all of them. We had fun when we were together. We should have been

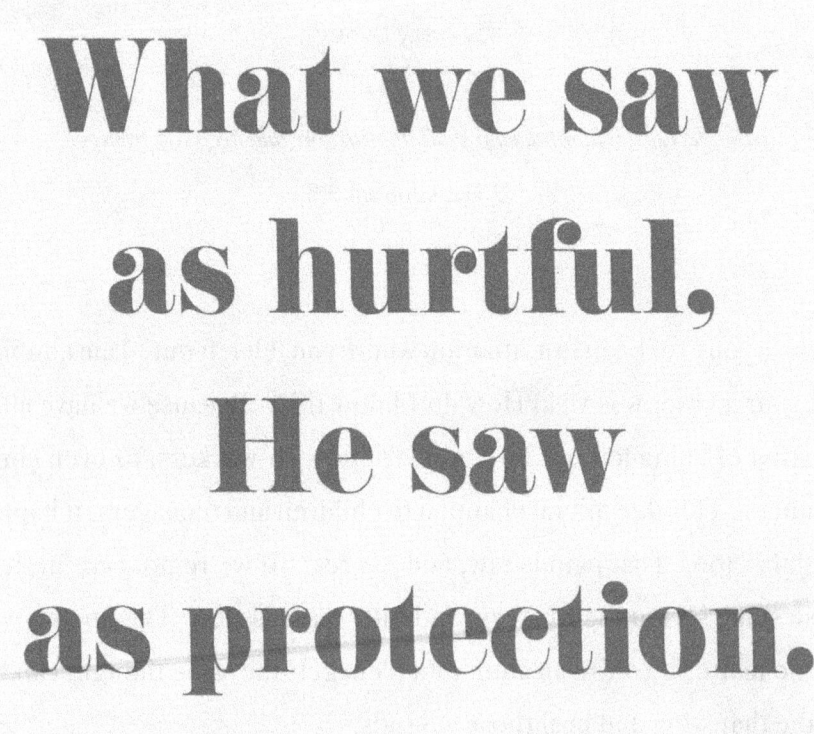

What we saw as hurtful, He saw as protection.

a close part of that group, but we weren't. Those couples often made plans without us. They would hang out and talk together and we wouldn't really be included. We were confused and discouraged. Then a few years later, some things happened, and we realized that we were very grateful that we had not been a close part of that group. Looking back, I can see that the Lord was protecting us. He knew us. He knew we desired to serve Him sincerely. He knew the standards we had and the way we wanted to live. He knew that we were different from that group. No one else knew it, but He did. What we saw as hurtful, He saw as protection. I am grateful now that we were left out.

How about when your teenager desires things because all their friends have them? What if these are good teenagers? What if they are from solid families? What if everything seems to be going okay with them having those things? Should you go against your own standards so your teenager doesn't feel left out? No! If the Lord is leading you to put up boundaries, keep them! I have seen so many young people ruined over certain things that seemed harmless in the beginning. Even good teenagers from good families who belong to good churches are getting swallowed up into these traps. I have seen parents who caved in on something and regretted it years later when their young adults turned away from everything they were taught. I have seen other parents who have stayed strong and their young adults are still walking closely with the Lord. Your teenager may feel left out because all of their friends have something they do not. It's going to hurt them to feel left out. It is going to hurt you to see them getting left out. However, I can assure you that if you stay strong and your teenager stays strong, one day they will be able to look back and see your hand of protection.

We should be constantly praying for wisdom and discernment so we avoid the desire to seek after something that the Lord does not want us to have. But sometimes the things we desire are not wrong and may even appear to be good things. This could be a job, ministry, friend, college, etc. However, if we try our best to gain these things and we end up being rejected from them, we need to consider the fact that it could just be the Lord shielding us from a direct hit or maybe He's shielding us from the destruction of someone else being hit. Either way, we need to remember that being left out could just be His loving hand of protection.

Here are just a few verses that can help us keep that perspective:

    Psalms 5:11 - But let all those that put their trust in thee rejoice: let them ever shout for joy, because thou defendest them: let them also that love thy name be joyful in thee.

    Psalm 32:7 - Thou art my hiding place; thou shalt preserve me from trouble; thou shalt compass me about with songs of deliverance. Selah.

    Psalm 121:5 - The Lord is thy keeper: the Lord is thy shade upon thy right hand.

    Psalm 40:11 - Withhold not thou thy tender mercies from me, O Lord: let thy lovingkindness and thy truth continually preserve me.

    Proverbs 2:11 - Discretion shall preserve thee, understanding shall keep thee:

    Isaiah 26:3 - Thou wilt keep him in perfect peace, whose mind is stayed on thee: because he trusteth in thee.

    Psalm 147:3 - He healeth the broken in heart, and bindeth up their wounds.

thankfulness

Date:

Scripture:

I'm thankful for...

On my heart...

Thankful for God's Guarantees

By Dixie Sasser

There shall not any man be able to stand before thee all the days of thy life: as I was with Moses, so I will be with thee: I will not fail thee, nor forsake thee.

Joshua 1:5

The author of this devotional has since passed on to be with the Lord. We want to publish this as a reminder that our ultimate future is settled in heaven. Mrs. Sasser lived a life of faithfulness to the Lord and her testimony lives on. She will be greatly missed on this earth.

My youngest son recently met with his financial advisor to discuss his mutual funds. The year 2022 was not a good year for stocks, and therefore, his returns were not good. His advisor assured him that the stocks would rebound and the returns would be better, but he could not give any guarantees. I am so thankful that God does give guarantees about our future. When God says, "I will," He means He will. It is a strong statement, and nothing can keep it from happening. I noticed three things in Joshua 1:5 to be thankful for about our future.

"I will be with thee." Our future is a sure future. God's presence will always be with us. We do not have to worry about going through this life alone. Matthew 28:20 says, "Lo, I am with you always." When hard times come, He will be with us. What an amazing promise!

"I will not fail thee." Our future is a secure future. God's power will always provide for us. We never have to worry about what tomorrow holds because God says that He will take care of us. He already sees tomorrow, so why do we worry so much over it? He knows what is best for us. The Great Depression was brought on because the market and the banks failed the people. People will fail us. We are not to put our trust in people but in God.

"Nor forsake thee." Our future is a safe future. God's protection will always be there for us. God does not get scared of the things that come into our lives; He stays by our side when others may run off. He will not allow Satan to destroy us because He is there with us to fight for us. We often try to run ahead of God and fight our own battles, and we get hurt and defeated. However, we are not destroyed and God did not leave us. He comes along and picks us up and mends our hurts. He loves us and encourages us to go on. The world may give up on us, but God never does.

Ever heard that old saying, "My future is so bright, I got to wear shades?" As Christians, our future is bright, but we do not have to wear shades. We can look straight at the light of our wonderful Lord and know that His guarantees are sure, secure, and safe. We can boldly go on to live for Him. Oh, how thankful we should be for His guarantees of our future!

thankfulness

Date:

Scripture:

I'm thankful for...

On my heart...

Thankful All the Time

By Julie Payne

In everything give thanks: for this is the will of God in Christ Jesus concerning you.
1 Thessalonians 5:18

Are you a thankful person? Sure, you may say "thank you" when you receive a gift or get a nice meal out . . . but what we need to realize is that this verse needs to be obeyed no matter what our situation is! Have you ever had someone tell you something as a warning, but it was something you would never dream of doing? Then the more you thought about it, the more it just hurt your feelings that they thought that of you. On the other hand, if this verse is obeyed, that battle with our flesh that is standing up for ourselves would be eliminated. We could just thank God for that warning! Remember that God knows us and sees the big picture of our life. So who are we to say what we would not do? "In everything give thanks," even when falsely accused.

There are also many different areas of life where we can be overwhelmed: burdens we're facing personally, trials we're going through, or not getting what we desire even if it's a good thing. This verse covers all these and more that come to your mind as well. So be thankful for that burden you bear; ask God to let it help you grow closer and depend more on Him.

Trials?! Yes! Be thankful for that hard time you're going through – even when it seems crazy and back-to-back. We don't always know what God is trying to purge out of our lives, test us to see where we really stand, or be an example for someone else's benefit. Oh, that we would want to pass God's test for whatever reason He has so His Glory can be seen in our lives.

Then, there are the things we desire. How can wanting a good thing be bad? Here is a quote: "Good can become the enemy of the best." In other words, every good thing may not be the best for us. So be thankful even when it seems something good is being withheld, and trust God's best for you.

"In everything give thanks," even in every area of being overwhelmed. God is all perfect, knowing, and powerful. He deserves our thanks for this. Even when we don't see it in our lives, it is still there. Romans 8:28 tells us that God is the Master of turning our bad to good, so just be thankful all the time! After all, it is the will of God for us to do this.

Challenge:

If you haven't already, read The Hiding Place, an autobiography by Corrie ten Boom with John and Elizabeth Sherrill. You will receive unforgettable inspiration from Corrie and Betsie ten Boom in obeying the verse "in everything give thanks."

thankfulness

Date:

Scripture:

I'm thankful for...

On my heart...

Effects of Thanklessness

By Kathy Lane

Bless the LORD, O my soul: And all that is within me, bless his holy name.
Psalm 103:1

I believe it is safe to assume that all of us have been taught at some point in our lives about the importance of being thankful. Those of us who had the privilege of growing up in Christian homes were taught not only to be mindful of God's physical blessings but spiritual blessings as well. But, on the flip side, are there adverse spiritual consequences for not having a spirit of thankfulness? A biblical reference is recalled – the children of Israel in the book of Exodus. After being miraculously delivered from their Egyptian bondage and personally witnessing God's countless miracles, it was only three days before God's people began to complain. "And the people murmured . . . ." This repeated response from the children of Israel became second nature for them. How could they complain so quickly after what God delivered them from? There are obviously various factors involved in such a carnal response, but one reason would be their ingratitude.

An unthankful spirit complains and nurtures a discontented heart and that leads down a dangerous path becoming poisonous to a believer. Let's not be so judgmental, because we all know we do the same thing whether we admit it or not. Do we realize that when we murmur and complain, we are in essence telling God that we deserve better than what He has given to us? Now, obviously, this does not mean we need to be thankful for everything; but I Thessalonians 5:18 commands us to be thankful *in* everything. A truly grateful heart is a humble heart that recognizes God's hand in every aspect of our life, and this becomes a natural result of spending time with the Lord.

When was the last time we expressed gratitude for things He has chosen to keep from us? Have we ever stopped to consider that God withholds certain things from us because, in His loving omniscience, He knows that we cannot handle them, and it would do us more harm than good? Have we, like the children of Israel, so easily forgotten what God has done for us? We have no grounds for boasting for anything we have, nor do we have grounds to think we deserve better. Apart from Christ, the only thing we have on our own is our sin – and that is certainly not anything to brag about! And the more blessings He compassionately chooses to bestow upon us, the more indebted we become to Him. A critical spirit is only one of the many side effects of ingratitude. The more we feed the insatiable spirit of ingratitude, the easier it becomes to be blinded by our arrogance and self-serving pride – which, remember, God hates (Proverbs 8:13; 16:5.) May the Lord convict our ungrateful hearts if anything besides the undeserving goodness of the Lord proceeds from our mouths.

thankfulness

Date:

Scripture:

I'm thankful for...

On my heart...

Say, "Thank You!"

By Callie Payne

That I may publish with the voice of thanksgiving, And tell of all thy wondrous works. LORD, I have loved the habitation of thy house, And the place where thine honor dwelleth.

Psalm 26:7-8

When I was young, my parents gave me an exciting birthday party! We didn't have a full-out "invite a bunch of friends over" party each year, but this was one of the milestone birthdays when I got to invite my friends over. There is a part of that day that I replay almost every birthday.

I remember starting to open gifts that everyone had brought over. I was so excited I tore into one gift right after the other. To my shame, I didn't even blink between each present. My poor mom had to keep reminding me to tell every person "thank you." You would think I'd have gotten the hint after the first few times, but no... I was so tunnel-visioned on what was in the next box or bag. After my party, I remember my parents sitting me down and letting me know how awful that feeling was for someone to have put thought, time, and money into each gift and someone not fully appreciating it.

Now, I don't tell this story just to embarrass myself (or my poor mother again, bless her heart.) But I think the principle applies in our everyday life.

"LORD, I have loved the habitation of thy house, And the place where thine honor dwelleth." (Psalm 26:8)

Church can be an anticipated part of our week. We get to spend time together in God's house, worshipping, serving alongside one another, praying together, and learning from God's Word. But I want to ask you - Are we working with our heads down in our ministry, so tunnel-visioned we can't see the blessings and gifts that are all around? God is blessing us in so many areas. If we're only focused on what we can gain in our ministry or the church service, we won't see those blessings. The opportunity to serve is something we should be thankful for!

Most likely, God has given you a church, a place to worship and serve Him. Don't take it for granted. When you're coming into the church, are you so focused on your role in the service or just getting to "your" seat that you miss the church family around you that God has blessed you with? When was the last time you thanked God for the people He's placed in your church? Don't let an ungrateful heart cause you to miss your blessings.

Just like all of my little friends were sitting there watching me open my presents with a "gimme, gimme" attitude, God is right there watching us receive gift after gift from Him with little to no acknowledgment of his goodness. Having a physical reminder to say, "Thank you" helps. Make a list of some obvious things that you might be taking for granted in your day-to-day life, ministry, and church. After you make that list, brag about the Lord to someone. As the verse states "tell of all" with a voice of thanksgiving. "That I may publish with the voice of thanksgiving, And tell of all thy wondrous works."

thankfulness

Date:

Scripture:

I'm thankful for...

On my heart...

Thankful for Who God Is

By Larissa Bell

And God said unto Moses, I AM THAT I AM: and he said, Thus shalt thou say unto the children of Israel, I AM hath sent me unto you.

Exodus 3:14

For several months now, I've really been meditating and dwelling on how thankful I am for Who God is. There is an amazing peace that passes all understanding when you get to know Him and truly realize that He is able to be Whomever and provide whatever you need. This peace develops as we read about Him in our Bibles and see Him working and moving in our lives. It grows as we go through struggles or trials, and we see Him provide and answer prayers. Our knowledge continues to deepen even when we go through calm periods where we rest and refresh our souls beside the still waters of His Word.

God has numerous names and attributes in the Bible, but one of my favorites is "I AM" (Exodus 3:14). The *Strong's Concordance* says this phrase is a verb (action) and means "to be" or "to exist." He is there; He always has been and always will be. Unlike the prophets of Baal in I Kings 18 who tried everything they could think of to get their god's attention, Elijah's (and my) One True God is omnipresent, omniscient, and omnipotent. He proved it when He heard and answered Elijah's 63-word prayer and sent fire down to consume "the burnt sacrifice, and the wood, and the stones, and the dust, and licked up the water that was in the trench" (I Kings 18:38.)

When I think of this name of God, I think, "I AM _____" (fill in the blank with what I need). Aren't you thankful that no matter what our need, we are able to find an attribute or character trait of God, a promise, or a story in the Bible to encourage our hearts to trust Him and have faith in that situation? I will list a few of the "I AM's" that I am most grateful for, but there is no room in a book to contain all that God is. As the old song, "The Love of God" so beautifully describes, if the ocean were filled with ink and the skies were the parchment, writing just the one attribute of love (God is love) would drain the ocean dry.

God is our Provider (Jehovah Jireh)

What peace we find in knowing God is able and willing to provide all our needs! Whether it's financial, health-related, emotional, or spiritual, God has the ability and means to meet those needs; He can be trusted and is faithful to fulfill His promises. Read the following verses:

- Philippians 4:19
- 2 Corinthians 9:8
- Matthew 6:25-33

God is our Counsellor (El Deah- God of Knowledge)

There are hundreds, if not thousands, of choices and decisions we make on a daily basis. Do I hit the snooze? What am I going to wear? What am I going to eat? How can I show love to my family? How can I be a better wife? How do I help my kids desire a close relationship with God? Who can I share Jesus with today? What passage should I read in my Bible . . . and that's just before 6 am! I find myself praying often throughout the day for wisdom and guidance, and I am thankful He is always listening. Sometimes God uses a recent sermon to help guide my decisions, and sometimes the answer can come from a song or a stranger. I marvel at the different ways God uses to counsel our hearts and direct our paths.

- Psalm 16:8
- Proverbs 12:15
- Judges 18: 5, 6 (I'm thankful too that we don't need a high priest anymore, but have direct access to the throne room of Heaven – Hebrews 4:14-16.)

God is our Healer (Jehovah-Rapha)

Whether it be a physical, mental, or spiritual health issue, God is our Healer. As our Creator and the Great Physician, He knows the body more intimately than all the scientists, doctors, and "subject matter experts" in the world combined. While He may allow painful health issues as He did for Job, He has also given us many principles and commands in the Bible that can improve all aspects of our health. Ask Him for wisdom and He will show you the resources you need to keep your mind and body able to serve Him. And when you feel like no one knows what you are going through or how much you're hurting, remember Jesus loves you so much that He left Heaven for you, taking upon Himself the pain, suffering, and temptations of living on earth. This ultimately led to a tortured death on the cross to bring you and me both abundant life on earth and the assurance of eternal life in Heaven without any physical, mental, or Spiritual illness!(John 10:10)

- Exodus 15:26
- Jeremiah 33:2-3, 6
- Isaiah 53: 4-5

I wish there was space to go on, as there are so many more "I AM's" than this. I do hope you'll start writing your own list down as you come across them in your Bible reading to encourage your heart and help you bask in thankfulness for the peace that passes all understanding.

thankfulness

Date:

Scripture:

I'm thankful for...

On my heart...

Giving Thanks - A Different Perspective

By Cherith Shiflett

And whatsoever ye do in word or deed, do all in the name of the Lord Jesus, giving thanks to God and the Father by him.

Colossians 3:17

What is gratitude exactly? Gratitude is a thankful appreciation for what you receive, whether tangible or intangible. Practicing gratitude is not only a command from God's Word but practicing gratitude has been known to alleviate stress, sadness, frustrations, doubt, fears, and the temptation to succumb to a victim mentality.

When we think about things we're grateful for, we can all list things like family, friends, health, jobs, food, house, cars, clothes, and on and on it goes. All of these things are great comforts in life and are deserving of thanksgiving. But are there other subjects we should consider when focusing on gratitude? What if your primary thanksgivings in life weren't the things that give you comfort?

What if you were thankful for that embarrassing mistake... because it gave you an opportunity to practice humility?

What if you were grateful for the person who is frustrating the daylights out of you... because this allows you to grow in patience?

What if you appreciate the "messy relationships" in your life... because this gives you an opportunity to lead others through trying times?

What if you're thankful for the fear you feel towards something challenging... because this allows you to act courageously?

Be thankful it was raining today...because now you don't have to go out and water your plants.

Be thankful you spilled that cup of coffee... because now you can make a fresh hot cup. (See, it even works with small, silly things.)

Instead of focusing on being thankful in general, be thankful in specifics. The right perspective of gratitude changes the lens through which we see circumstances in our lives.

It's hard to begrudge something or someone you just expressed thankfulness for. It's hard to throw a pity party for yourself about the things you just told the Lord you were grateful for.

I know it's hard to always find a "silver lining," but if we change our perspective towards gratitude it should quickly become a habit.

Thanksgiving is an expression of joy, not because of what God provides but because He is the Provider.

For some, gratitude is easier than others. I know some individuals that just radiate gratitude with a genuine heart. (It really is contagious when you're around them.) Sadly, a lot of believers are not marked with this trait. We have the most to be thankful for, yet you'd never know it by our conversation, our attitude, or our face.

Gratitude isn't something that can be cultivated on our own. Think of that individual I mentioned above - always grateful - what does their walk with the Lord look like? Gratitude overflows from a heart that is in love with Jesus and sold out to His service. When we love Jesus with our whole being, we cannot help but live with a thankful heart that seeks to worship our Saviour in all we do.

thankfulness

Date:

Scripture:

I'm thankful for...

On my heart...

Can I Be Trusted?

By Victoria Kiker

In every thing give thanks: for this is the will of God in Christ Jesus concerning you.
I Thessalonians 5:18

Dr. Helen Roseveare was an English medical missionary in the mid-1950s and 1960s. Her work in the African Congo took her to many poor, desperately needy people. She began sharing the Gospel with the Congolese, helping to build hospitals and clinics, train nurses, and treating many sick with much needed medical aid. In 1960, the Congo became independent of Belgium and in 1964, civil war broke out. All the medical facilities she had helped build were destroyed and civil unrest began to quickly rise.

Helen, along with ten other missionaries, was soon placed under house arrest, then later taken by rebel forces and kept prisoner for five months. She endured multiple brutal beatings and eventually was horrifically raped by her captors. She said the Lord came to her during that time and asked, "Can you thank Me for trusting you with this even

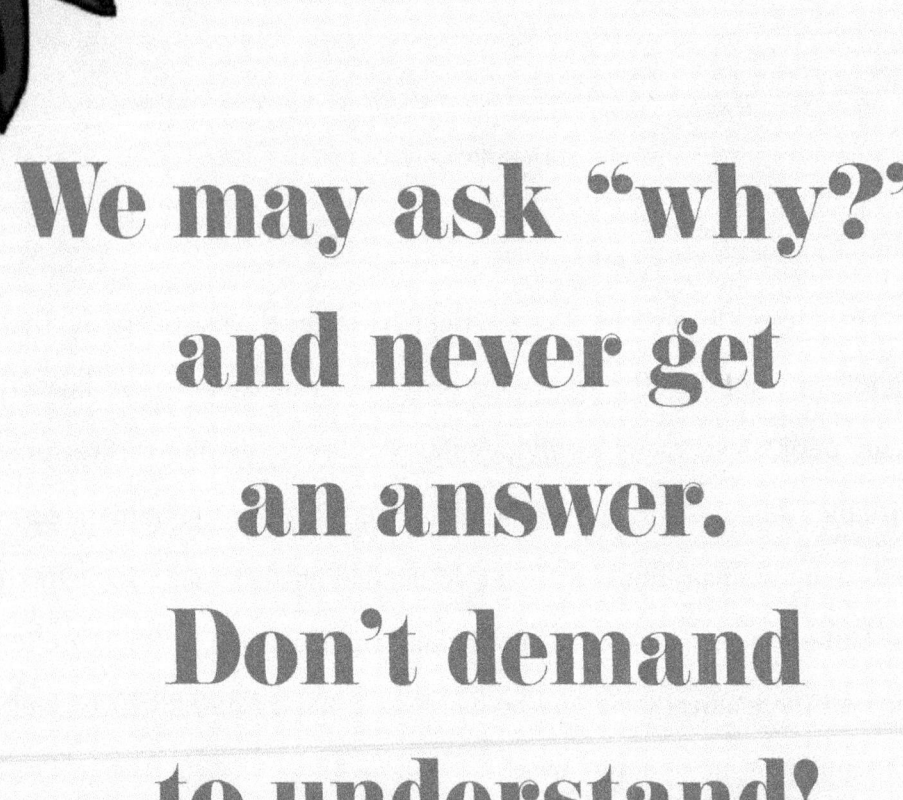

We may ask "why?" and never get an answer. Don't demand to understand!

if I never tell you why?" Her immediate thought was, "No, I cannot!" How could she be thankful for this? It had been too much; the pain, torture, and humiliation had gone too far. Helen felt (as we all would) that such atrocities should never come to one who was faithfully serving the Lord. After all, she had given up so much to reach the very ones who had wounded her so deeply. Finally, Helen surrendered her pain to her Father. She thanked Him for trusting her and was immediately filled with the wondrous, unexplainable peace of God.

After Helen was released she said, "One word became unbelievably clear, and that word was privilege. He didn't take away pain or cruelty or humiliation. No! It was all there, but now it was altogether different. It was with Him, for Him, in Him. He was actually offering me the inestimable privilege of sharing in some little way the edge of the fellowship of His suffering. In the weeks of imprisonment that followed and in the subsequent years of continued service, looking back, one has tried to 'count the cost,' but I find it all swallowed up in privilege. The cost suddenly seems very small and transient in the greatness and permanence of the privilege."

The question the Lord asked of Dr. Roseveare convicted me after listening to her testimony. There will be times in our walk with Christ that He will allow difficulties and trials to come. We may ask "why?" and never get an answer. Don't demand to understand! As difficult as it is, thank Him. Thank Him for trusting you with your situation. Think about that; He trusted you. Like Dr. Roseveare, consider what a true privilege it is to be Christ's, to be counted worthy of His fellowship. So, may I pose the question to you and me: can we be trusted? It's incredibly easy to be thankful when days are sunny and life is comfortable, but the tide will turn; it always does. Inevitably, one day those clear, blue skies will turn gray and stormy. When it does, can you be thankful that God trusted you with the storm? He is worthy to be thanked, despite our situation. Dear reader, we know that our mighty God can be trusted, but can you? Can I? I sincerely pray so.

"There really is no cost, only the privilege of serving the King of kings." – Dr. Helen Roseveare

Note: Look up video interviews with Dr. Roseveare. You will be encouraged. She's written several books as well.

thankfulness

Date:

Scripture:

I'm thankful for...

On my heart...

About The Authors

Each author has been handpicked because of their testimony for Christ. God has gifted each writer with incredibly versatile perspectives of the Christian life. These godly ladies come from all walks of life including pastor's wives and daughters, missionary wives, church staff ladies, and faithful church members. Their written words of wisdom are sure to bless your heart.

To know more about our writers please visit:
thehighlyfavouredlife.com/our-story

Check Out
The Highly Favoured Life

on

and
thehighlyfavouredlife.com

www.ingramcontent.com/pod-product-compliance
Lightning Source LLC
Chambersburg PA
CBHW072025060426
42449CB00035B/2649